A CHRISTIAN APPROACH TO LOSS

LEAVING GRIEF BEHIND
✧ DEVOTIONAL ✧

FIONA SEM

Leaving Grief Behind: A Christian Approach to Loss Devotional
Copyright © 2025 by Fiona Sem.

All rights reserved.

No part of this publication may be reproduced, distributed, or transmitted in any form or by any means, including photocopying, recording, or other electronic or mechanical methods, without the prior written permission of the publisher or author, except in the case of brief quotations embodied in critical reviews and certain other noncommercial uses permitted by U.S. copyright law.

All Scripture quotations, unless otherwise indicated, are taken from the *New International Version*.

ISBN: 979-8-28723808-7

Printed in the United States of America.

First Printing Edition 2025.

Photos by Abby Galindo Photography.

www.fionasem.com

TABLE OF CONTENTS

INTRODUCTION..5
DAY 1: EVERLASTING JOY..7
DAY 2: THE LOST IS FOUND..11
DAY 3: GRIEVING LOSS..15
DAY 4: RAGING WATERS...19
DAY 5: EMOTIONAL INTELLIGENCE............................23
DAY 6: FORGIVING GOD..27
DAY 7: INNER-HEALING PRAYER.................................31
DAY 8: KNOWING GOD'S CHARACTER.......................35
DAY 9: JESUS WEPT...39
DAY 10: GOD IS GOOD..43
DAY 11: MADE WITH A PURPOSE................................47
DAY 12: HEAVEN AND EARTH 51

CONCLUSION...55

INTRODUCTION

Welcome to the *Leaving Grief Behind Devotional*! This devotional was thoughtfully crafted as a supplement to the book *Leaving Grief Behind: A Christian Approach to Loss* and as a way to dive deeper into studying Scripture and applying it to daily life. Over the course of the next twelve days, this devotional will follow the book chapter by chapter. The *Leaving Grief Behind Devotional* includes special extended content and concepts beyond the book, as well as additional Bible verses, questions, and space for note-taking. I really hope you enjoy this devotional (either on your own or with friends!) and that it draws you closer to God.

DAY 1:
EVERLASTING JOY

Joy isn't something you have to search for. It's not found in a new car, new clothes, or precious jewels. It's not found in status or fame, friends or even family. Joy isn't something you have to look for because joy is already here.

We were gifted joy the very moment God came down to earth in the form of man. He was called Immanuel or "God with us." The Son of Man, God incarnate, was sent for us to receive joy.

Supernatural joy reveals itself in the Christmas story—God, a baby born in a manger. Simply put, joy is in the normal, ordinary, everyday moments of our lives, as well as in the unexpected ones.

True joy is rooted in hope—the hope that troubles are only momentary. Joy is greater than simple satisfaction and beyond fleeting pleasure and the pursuit of happiness. True joy is a deep well that can be found even in the middle of despair, the midst of pain, and the worst of circumstances. Joy hopes for the future.

God is the beginning and the end. What you're going through, He's already been through and is waiting on the other side. When He came to earth, He already knew what He was going to do way before we even saw it coming. He knew He was going to be beaten and ridiculed and bloodied on our behalf. He knew He was going to suffer death on the cross for our sins. The Savior had come so our battle could be won.

BIBLE VERSES

Luke 2:10-11

Isaiah 61:1-7

QUESTIONS:

1. What kinds of things bring you momentary happiness versus deep joy? Is there a difference between happiness and joy?

2. Was there ever a time when you had to steward joy even when you didn't feel like it?

3. Can joy be stewarded immediately or must it be grown in waiting?

NOTES

NOTES

DAY 2:
THE LOST IS FOUND

Have you ever felt undervalued at work? Like no matter how hard you work, it just seems like all of your efforts go unrecognized. If you were to leave, no one would care and someone would replace you soon enough.

Perhaps, you feel unseen in your family—outshined by the golden child (the football star, the math whiz, the musical prodigy, etc.). Maybe you're a middle child, and you just feel lost in the crowd.

It is easy to feel like a number—to feel like no one cares. But God cares. God sees you. God values you. No matter where you are, what state you're in, or what you're going through, God loves you.

In Luke 15, Jesus tells three parables describing this kind of love. The first is about the shepherd who leaves the ninety-nine to find the one lost sheep. The second is about the poor woman who searches desperately for her lost coin. The third is about the father who threw a feast for his prodigal son when he finally returned home.

God loves you so much, and He is running after you. He's coming to rescue you and make a way where there seems to be no way. "For this son of mine was dead and is alive again; he was lost and is found" (Luke 15:24).

BIBLE VERSES

Luke 15:4-7

Luke 15:8-10

Luke 15:11-32

QUESTIONS:

1. How does it feel to be fully known and fully loved by God?

2. Has there ever been a time when you felt misunderstood by everyone? When only God understood you?

3. How does God meet you right where you are? Is it a place, state of mind, capacity?

NOTES

NOTES

DAY 3:

GRIEVING LOSS

As Christians, we have the hope of eternal life. Jesus paid the price for our sins, laid down his life in exchange for ours, rose from the grave and conquered death so that we could live.

Yet, when someone in our life dies, we can feel the opposite of victorious. A common phrase people say in church is "God doesn't waste a hurt." But sometimes, hurt can feel wasted with no purpose.

Why do we struggle so much with the concept of death? I think we have such a hard time letting go because we were meant for so much more. Humanity was created with an eternal purpose.

How can we be more prepared for death? By living. We should live like eternal life starts now. We don't have to fear death. We're still here and here for a purpose. Just take a breath and live.

BIBLE VERSES

Ecclesiastes 3:1-14

Romans 6:23

Romans 8:38-39

QUESTIONS:

1. Would you say you struggle with the concept of death? How have you handled grief and loss in the past? How about now?

2. What does it mean to live your life like eternity starts now? What does that look like for you?

3. What matters and what doesn't in eternity?

NOTES

NOTES

DAY 4:

RAGING WATERS

"Surely the rising of the mighty waters will not reach them (Psalms 32:6 NIV)." I love this verse because life can make you feel like you're drowning—drowning in work, chores, bills. Just one thing after another in a cycle that never lets up. It's just too much. It feels like you're sinking, failing miserably, and just trying to get by—just trying to survive.

There are three stories in the Bible about this feeling of drowning: 1) Jonah and the Whale, 2) Jesus Calms the Storm, and 3) Jesus Walks on Water.

From these passages, we know that Jesus is the calm before, after, and in the middle of the storm. He takes what is stormy and makes it still. He takes what is turbulent and turns it into solid ground. Not only is Jesus the one who calms the winds and waves, but He's the one who can stand on top of them!

Even when you feel like you can't take another step, Jesus is taking steps towards you. Jesus in the middle of the storm that you are facing right now. Even when you're drowning in grief and just trying to survive, the mighty waters will not reach you.

BIBLE VERSES

Psalms 32:6

Jonah 2:1-10

Mark 4:35-41

Matthew 14:22-33

QUESTIONS:

1. Think about a time when God has come through for you even when your faith has failed.

2. What in your life right now feels currently too much to handle on your own?

3. In your own words, how do these three stories reassure you that the mighty waters will not reach you? How can you believe for the future?

NOTES

NOTES

DAY 5:
EMOTIONAL INTELLIGENCE

Emotional intelligence is understanding where your emotions come from and the purpose that they serve. Because when you are aware of your feelings and actually feel them, it becomes less likely for those feelings to build up into outbursts. Emotional intelligence is about managing your feelings (i.e., happy, sad, angry, afraid, ashamed) in an appropriate manner.

I believe that when God created us, He created our emotions. These feelings cannot be ignored. They cannot be separated from our flesh. Yet, in our humanity, we can choose to separate our emotions from sin. God has given us the ability to steward emotional intelligence to overcome even the worst of circumstances.

BIBLE VERSES

John 11:35

1 Corinthians 10:23

Ephesians 4:26

QUESTIONS:

1. Since God created our emotions, do you think that it is good to feel them? Use Bible verses to explain your reasoning.

2. How aware are you of your emotions? How well do you manage your emotions?

3. What does the Bible say about feeling happy, sad, angry, afraid, and ashamed?

NOTES

NOTES

DAY 6:
FORGIVING GOD

King David is often known for his many songs in the Book of Psalms. Some of his writings are known as lament poems —authentic prayers that are reflective of David's close relationship with God. David often cried out to the Lord. There was nothing that he felt like he couldn't share. Prayer was a way for David to be open and honest with God about everything he was going through, and God was a friend that was listening to all of David's feelings and frustrations. Where David was weak, God was strong.

When life is tough, we fall into the temptation of blaming God. However, sin separates God and man, and blame severs an authentic prayer life. Yet, to forgive God for the ups and downs of life is to release control to its true author. We can't change the past, but we can allow God to come in and write us a new future. When we give up the desire to write our own stories, God becomes the solution to life's problems. God uses vulnerability to redeem situations.

BIBLE VERSES

Psalms 142:1-7

Psalms 51:1-19

QUESTIONS:

1. Compare and contrast Psalms 142 and Psalms 51. How does David's prayer life showcase authenticity with God?

2. How would you describe your prayer life? What does your prayer life say about your relationship with God?

3. Is there something in your past that still doesn't quite sit right with you? Is there something or someone that is holding you back from forgiveness? Pray to God about the feelings you are feeling surrounding certain people or situations.

NOTES

NOTES

DAY 7:
INNER–HEALING PRAYER

Inner-healing prayer is a type of prayer that can be used for physical, mental, emotional, social, and spiritual healing. Not only that, but this type of prayer can also be a prayer for repentance. Through inner-healing prayer, Jesus is invited into a situation to do a fully transformative work from the inside out.

James 5:15-16 puts it best:

"And the prayer offered in faith will make the sick person well; the Lord will raise them up. If they have sinned, they will be forgiven. Therefore confess your sins to each other and pray for each other so that you may be healed. The prayer of a righteous person is powerful and effective."

Although inner-healing prayers can be prayed on your own, there is power in community and having others pray over you as well.

Just as in Jesus's ministry, miracles can still happen today. Don't stop praying even if change doesn't happen as quickly as you would like it to or how you would like it to. God hears us when we pray. His presence and power is always made available to us. Not only do we have access to healing but to the forgiveness of our sins.

BIBLE VERSES

James 5:15-16

Matthew 18:18-20

Luke 11:1-13

QUESTIONS:

1. Have you experienced inner-healing before? If so, reflect on a time when God healed you, and thank God for what He has done in your life.

2. Is there something in your life currently that might require inner-healing prayer? Take some time today to spend in prayer with the God who heals and performs miracles.

3. Is there someone in your life that you feel like you can open up and share what you're struggling with? Who can you pray together with?

NOTES

NOTES

DAY 8:
KNOWING GOD'S CHARACTER

The Bible is called the Word of God because it's literally the living, breathing words of God. The Bible is not just any book. The Word is alive. When we devote ourselves to reading the Bible (even when we don't fully understand), God promises us that He will make Himself known. Jeremiah 29:13 (NIV) says, "You will seek me and find me when you seek me with all your heart." God wants us to know Him.

During my darkest moments and in times of despair and distress, God lifted me up and spoke truth over my circumstance. Even though a situation seems hopeless and you're staring death right in the face, you can know that God will be there.

Just as God spoke the universe and humanity into existence, God can bring dead things to life. The Bible is alive though it may seem like an ordinary book. When you trust God's Word, you can have hope for every situation because you know who God is.

BIBLE VERSES

John 1:1

2 Samuel 22:31

Isaiah 55:10-11

QUESTIONS:

1. What does it mean to seek God with all of your heart? Does it seem like something that is hard to do?

2. How is God speaking to you through today's word? What is He revealing about His character?

3. What is one Bible verse that you've memorized and meditated on for when trials, tests, and temptations come? What godly truth can you hold onto?

NOTES

NOTES

DAY 9:
JESUS WEPT

Jesus wept. It's the shortest verse in the entire Bible, but it says so much about the character of Jesus. Although He was fully God and fully man, He was still able to feel.

But why would Jesus feel the need to cry if He had access to the power of resurrection? If we take a look at John 11 where this verse comes from, the story of Lazarus's resurrection will explain.

First, Jesus loved Lazarus. The Bible says that Jesus was deeply moved in spirit and troubled by Lazarus's death. Jesus genuinely grieved the death of His good friend.

Second, Jesus displayed empathy by grieving alongside others. Jesus also cared for Lazarus's sisters. Mary and Martha were loyal to His ministry and often followed Jesus around. Throughout the Bible, Jesus consistently showed empathy by defending the women and raising them to higher positions in society. Because of His love, Jesus would be with His friends in their grief.

Third, Jesus wept so that we may believe even in the midst of grief. Jesus recognized grief as part of the process and waited to perform the resurrection miracle. Jesus didn't rush the solution because faith grows in the waiting.

Struggles in life make us more reliant on God. It increases our faith to believe that what is seen is not what will be because all things are possible for God. Miracles are possible for God. He can even raise the dead to life.

BIBLE VERSES

John 11:1-44

2 Corinthians 1:3-7

Psalms 71:20-21

QUESTIONS:

1. Have you ever cried with someone you loved? When it comes to crying, how good are you at expressing similar types of emotions?
2. There are many things in life that we can grieve over whether that's the death of a loved one or a great season that has ended or things not going the way that we hoped. How can trouble and hardship push you to rely more on God?
3. Why is it so hard to wait for a miracle? How has waiting increased your faith?

NOTES

NOTES

DAY 10:
GOD IS GOOD

If God is good, then why do good people sometimes have it so bad? If we take a look at Job, we might ask, "Why did he deserve any of this?" Maybe, there isn't a reason—aside from the fact that the current world in which we live in was not made to be free of suffering. It is good but not perfect.

We all face struggles. Even Jesus suffered on this earth. Maybe, the story of Job just goes to say that even though Job lost everything—literally everything—even he made it out alright. When Job was at his very worst, he still chose to see God's goodness.

When we know who God is, we can trust in Him with confidence. This knowledge of God's goodness is beyond knowing. Faith is a walk revealed through experience.

BIBLE VERSES

Genesis 3:1-24

Matthew 7:9-11

Matthew 16:13-19

QUESTIONS:

1. Imagine going through what Job experienced (i.e., losing your fortune, losing your children, dealing with a painful disease, etc.). Would you still be able to say God is good? Why?

2. What are some practical things you can do to surrender your definition of good and evil for God's definition? How can you surrender your will for God's will?

3. Who do you say God is? Take some time to journal how you have personally experienced different aspects of God's character.

NOTES

NOTES

DAY 11:
MADE WITH A PURPOSE

Loss can make you feel like life is purposeless, and the enemy tells us the lie that we should feel ashamed of who we are at our very core. But God has made us with purpose.

1. I am a child of God, and I am loved by God.

2. I am beautifully and wonderfully made. From my very creation, God knew me inside and out. At the very core of who I am, God chose me.

3. I am coheir with Christ. I can inherit eternal life and share in the treasures of heaven. God wants to give me a good life.

You can't change the past, but you can decide how to move forward. Even if life didn't turn out the way we had hoped, anything is possible with God.

BIBLE VERSES

Ephesians 1:4-5

Psalms 139:13-14

Romans 8:14-17

QUESTIONS:

1. How is what God says about you contradictory to what the world says? To what you say about yourself?

2. If there was one thing that you could change about yourself what would that be? Why?

3. Do you feel fully known and fully loved by God? In community?

NOTES

NOTES

DAY 12:
HEAVEN AND EARTH

How can we say that God is good after loss? When nothing makes sense? When we pray for something and it doesn't come true? What are we supposed to do then? When we pray for God's protection over our little ones, when we pray that cancer and sickness wouldn't overtake our loved ones, when we pray to experience the good life here and now and overwhelmingly see hopelessness, deep sorrow, and death all around? What do we do when we pray for something and it doesn't happen?

Although earth is imperfect and full of pain, heaven is perfect and full of joy. There will be eternal joy in heaven—the joy of being with God forever and ever. Yes, God wants us to have the desires of our hearts and experience glimpses of heaven on earth. But, even if we do not see our dreams come to pass here on earth, there will forever be the perfect hope of heaven. And it will be beyond whatever we could've imagined, hoped, or dreamed.

BIBLE VERSES

John 16:22

Revelation 21:4

Habakkuk 3:17-18

QUESTIONS:

1. How do you imagine, hope, and dream a perfect heaven would be like? Take some time to read what the Bible says about heaven, pray, and journal.

2. Do you feel ready for a life in heaven? Or are there still things on earth that you are holding onto?

3. Are you okay with life not being perfect here on earth?

NOTES

NOTES

CONCLUSION

You did it! Thanks for investing time in studying the Word of God and what it means in your personal relationship with Him. I pray that you continue to walk in intimacy with God–trusting in times of grief, receiving life even after death, and accessing eternal joy. Thanks for coming along for the journey!

FIND FIONA SEM ON:

fionasem.com

Made in the USA
Monee, IL
12 August 2025

23181838R00036